The
Monday
Revolution
Essentials

"This edition builds brilliantly on *The Monday Revolution*, offering insights that are immediately actionable for any business. A must-read for anyone navigating today's complex business landscape. Highly recommended."

– TIMO BOLDT, CEO AND FOUNDER, GOUSTO

First published in 2025 by David Mansfield,
in partnership with Whitefox Publishing Ltd
themondayrevolution.com
www.wearewhitefox.com
Copyright © David Mansfield, 2025
EU GPSR Authorised Representative
LOGOS EUROPE, 9 rue Nicolas Poussin, 17000, LA ROCHELLE, France
E-mail: Contact@logoseurope.eu
ISBN 978-1-917523-24-0
Also available as an eBook
ISBN 978-1-917523-25-7

Cartoons © Pearsall Cartoons
Icons from www.flaticon.com
Edited by Jill Sawyer
Designed and typeset by maru studio G.K.
Cover design by maru studio G.K.
Project management by Whitefox Publishing

DAVID MANSFIELD

The
Monday
Revolution

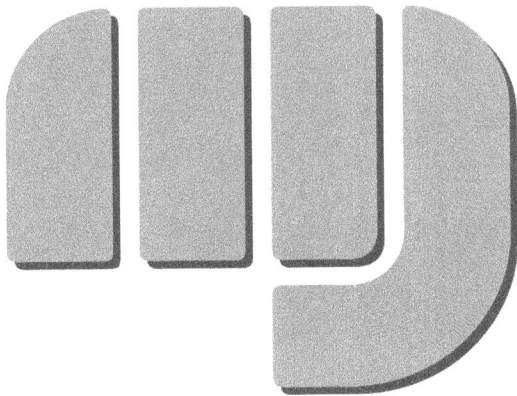

Essentials

Simple Actions for Significant Results

Contents

BEHIND
THE
BOOK:
THE IDEA

I've written this edition as a follow-up to *The Monday Revolution*, which was published in 2020. It features daily actions that anyone can take to immediately improve their business.

I had a great response to the previous book and many people told me the action points were the most useful part. So I've collected the most relevant, along with many new ones and illustrated each chapter with a cartoon to help get the message across!

The original idea aimed to cut through noise, eliminate procrastination, and prioritise actions to get things done. And since then, the world has become even more complex and the need for focus even greater.

Everyone I meet seems busier than ever and increasingly worried about their growing to-do list. Instead of taking simple actions, we are drawn to complicated solutions and multiple options. This book suggests how we spend our time is worth a second look.

The ideas are based on my personal experience, and understandably, you may not agree with everything. You'll have your own examples of what has worked, which is perfectly fine. Ignore what doesn't resonate and move on to parts of the book where you might find a new or alternative perspective.

Taking simple actions to achieve significant results can help make time your friend rather than your enemy. If this book offers a few answers and prompts some reflection on what you're doing and why, I'll consider the time writing it well spent!

PEOPLE

1
Who's in charge around here?

Good leader, bad leader

A good leader understands that visibility is crucial. You can't lead if your team is unaware of who you are and what you represent. It's essential to take the time to engage with your people, understand their challenges and see how they manage their responsibilities.

Being a visible and accessible leader isn't optional: it must be integrated into your routine. Leadership is genuinely tested during challenging times, not just when everything is going well. Be present when it matters most.

OK, SO... THAT'S THE GOOD NEWS. SALLY HERE WILL DELIVER THE BAD NEWS... I'M OFF TO LUNCH.

Leadership is about recognising when to be visible. You can't lead an organisation unless people know who you are and what you stand for.

Spend time with the front line. Get to know individuals and how they spend their day. Your direct reports may protest that this is undermining them. Make sure it isn't, but don't let that possibility stop you doing it.

Make a commitment to being a visible, in-touch leader by building a plan into your working week. Being too busy and not making the effort to stay in touch simply isn't good enough. But don't steal the limelight or all the glory either!

Showing up when there's good news is easy. Showing up when there's bad news tests leadership. Don't fail, because when it really counts, everyone will notice if you were missing.

2
The horse's mouth

Communication from you

Effective communication is at the core of leadership. It's not enough to just speak. You must engage, especially during challenging times. Be present, clear and proactive in sharing information with your people.

By setting expectations for communication and sticking to them, you create trust and accountability. Leaders who are known for communicating well stand out, building stronger teams and more resilient organisations.

Acknowledge that leadership and communication are inseparable. Recognise that in tough times communication needs to be stepped up – regardless of whether it's to your people or those outside. Do not disappear when people expect to see you.

Never assume there's no real need to explain because people know what's going on. They don't, and by saying so, you're using that as a reason for not standing up and doing the right thing.

Agree with your team what regular communication should look like. Draw up a plan, tell people what to expect and deliver it. It really isn't that hard.

*Being known for good communication
is a great accolade and can really set
you apart from others who choose
to avoid this important leadership
responsibility and skill.*

3
Join us, there's a Pret next door

Hiring

First impressions count, and that starts with your company's image. When creating job descriptions, be clear and dynamic – vague roles won't attract top talent. Always ask candidates for evidence to back up their claims: if they can't deliver, it's a red flag.

Implement a thorough hiring process with tests and practical exercises. The best candidates will appreciate your attention to detail and your commitment to finding the right fit.

First impressions are important.
Make sure your image is
the best it can be.

Describe the role in a clear, positive and dynamic way. If it reads like a job written by somebody who doesn't understand what they're doing, you might miss the opportunity to bring in the right talent.

Ask candidates to provide evidence to support their claims. If they can't, don't hire them. And do your own digging.

Have a proven process for employing people. Use tests, psychologists and practical exercises. Good people won't mind.

In fact, they'll be impressed with your diligence.

4
Sticks and carrots

Pay and reward

Make your job offers irresistible – they should stand out from the crowd. Build a reputation as a company that values its people, both within and outside the organisation.

Stay ahead of market trends and ensure your top performers are rewarded so you don't risk losing them. Design performance-based pay schemes that align with your appraisals. Pay should reflect the behaviours you want to promote, so avoid rewarding actions that don't mirror your goals.

OK, WELL THAT DIDN'T WORK... LET'S TRY THE CARROT...

When hiring, make your advertisement,

invitation, head-hunter call or whatever

more appealing than everyone else's.

This will not be hard.

Promote the positives of what you do inside and outside the organisation. Be one of those companies you've heard of but rarely worked for: "No point in approaching her, too well looked after."

Establish market demand and reward
for all your key people. Review their
contracts. Keep ahead or you'll
lose them. Design a salary-based
performance-related pay scheme for
everybody. And if you don't know what
they do or why they're here,
make a saving.

Ensure appraisals and rewards are aligned. You're paying for behaviour in all its forms. Don't appraise people for one thing and pay them for doing something else.

5
Who's made the cut?

Building high-performance teams

Attracting top talent starts with making your company and roles irresistible. Use a thorough selection process with tasks and expert input. Look below the surface, as past challenges often fuel future success.

High-performing teams thrive with high-performing leadership, with competitive pay and rewards tied to both team and individual achievements. Be the company everyone aspires to work for, and the best talent will naturally gravitate toward you.

Everything from company image to the job described needs to be compelling. To attract the right people, you need to be attractive.

The selection process needs to be rigorous and appropriate to what's required. Set tasks. Use outside expertise and tools. Identify complementary skills. Remember, experiencing adversity and failure are often hidden drivers of future success.

High-performance teams need high-performance leadership. Create the right environment and provide competitive pay and performance rewards linked directly to team and personal achievement.

Be a company that everybody aspires to work for and great talent will be attracted to your organisation.

NUMBERS

6
Numbers, it's a game you know

Measurement matters

Cash is the lifeblood of any business – without enough,
you're at risk. Stay on top of your finances with tools like
a daily cash flow tracker. Ensure your reports are both
accurate and actionable.

If sales dip, don't hesitate to cut back on spending, negotiate
better terms or put projects on hold. Don't wait for things
to get better on their own. Take decisive action before the
situation gets out of hand.

Recognise that, ultimately, having no cash is the only reason companies fail. Avoid running out of cash by staying very, very close to the numbers. A company I work with has a daily cash flow tracker. Not a bad idea.

Invest in financial resources you trust and ensure your management reports match the business needs. Always remain in control of your cash.

If sales dip beyond your expectation, have a back-up plan ready. Defer expenditure. Negotiate better payment terms. Put "exciting" projects on hold. In extreme circumstances, be prepared to fire people.

Most companies leave it far too late to take action, relying on "I hope it gets better." By the time they bite the bullet the situation has started to spiral out of control. Don't be one of those.

7
Pass the spreadsheet

Data. Wood. Data. Trees. Data

Too much data can overwhelm and hinder progress. Don't track everything just because you can. Focus on actionable insights that give you a competitive edge. You may have access to the same data as everyone else, but it's how you use it that counts.

Regularly review your data, streamline your reports and focus on what truly drives results. Cut down on unnecessary key performance indicators (KPIs) and reassess your objectives and key results (OKRs). Simplicity is the key to success.

Acknowledge that too much information creates confusion, overwhelms people and can restrict productivity and growth. Don't measure everything just because you can.

Clever analysis of data is undoubtedly a competitive edge, providing it's actionable. In a world that shares the same information, it's what you do with it that your competitors don't that counts.

Regularly review your information supply chain. What reports are prepared, what do you need and what are you doing with them? Less is definitely more.

Reduce the amount of KPIs. You know you've already too many to make sense of all of them. And while you're there, look at OKRs too.

8
I'm not paying that

The price is right?

Think like a retailer when pricing your products – they are masters at understanding the psychology behind what to charge. Look for opportunities to disrupt with creative pricing strategies.

Focus on building recurring revenue to transform project-based income into consistent monthly cash flow. Identify and halt loss leaders and vanity projects that waste resources: they are a drain on your business.

Every little helps us.

I LOVE IT! ...HOW WOULD IT LOOK IF WE DROPPED THE 'US'?

Examine pricing data for your products and services and think like a retailer. They understand pricing psychology better than most.

How could you be a price disrupter through more innovative and creative pricing? Amazon is a great source of ideas that work.

Recurring revenue is the holy grail.
What can you do to turn project income
into sustainable monthly income?

Identify loss leaders, low margins and vanity projects. Be realistic about them ever paying their way. Better to ditch them now than later.

9
Black holes

Disappearing money and how to avoid it

Don't skimp on investing in top-tier finance talent. Verify their expertise and offer competitive compensation. Place them at the core of strategy and operations, giving them full visibility into the business.

Hold them accountable for all financial data, as unforeseen challenges will arise. Keep a sharp eye on cash flow, as this is more critical to your business operations than profits or earnings before interest, taxes, depreciation and amortisation (EBITDA).

Don't cut corners when hiring finance people. Find the best you can, validate with supporting evidence and pay them well.

Sit them at the top of the company. Involve them in strategy and operations – they need to know everything. Make it clear they can go anywhere and ask anything, of anybody, including you.

Ensure they recognise they are ultimately accountable for all financial evidence. In the business universe the unexpected happens and black holes will appear.

Always understand cash flow. Free cash flow is what you have left when you've sold your product and paid your costs. This is far more important than profits or EBITDA.

SELLING

10
A sales story or two

No sales, no business

Ideas are only valuable when your audience recognises their worth. Customise your offer for each buyer, as one-size-fits-all doesn't work in business-to-business (B2B) sales. Research your target market and activity, using public data to uncover opportunities.

In meetings, prioritise understanding the client's unsolved problems and tailor your solution accordingly. Always leave with clear next steps. When networking, resist the temptation to sell right away – listening is key to securing a follow-up discussion.

?

Information and ideas are gold if you have something that others will perceive as valuable. Position your offer in the unique context of the buyer. In B2B selling, one size never fits all.

?

Spend time looking at the target company's activity, profile and market. Work out what you could provide. This may just cost you time. Available public data highlighting trends could be all you need.

?

Having secured a meeting, uncover the client's unsolved problems and carefully match your proposition. Always leave with agreed actions and next steps. Always.

?

If you're networking, listen and say enough to agree a follow-up. Resist the temptation to hit the sales pitch button there and then.

11
Right message, right place, right time

Making the most of marketing money

Marketing expenditure should never be viewed as a luxury. During tough times, it's often the first to be cut, but if approached strategically it can be a key driver of sales.

Treat marketing spend as an investment that requires measurable returns and be flexible enough to adjust your plans in response to market shifts. Regularly assess your marketing strategy for greater accountability and to ensure everything spent delivers tangible results.

And that's for your fun little marketing project...

BUDGET

Is marketing money seen as a nice-to-have or an essential driver of sales? In tricky times are these the first budgets to go? Perhaps there lies the answer.

📢

Do you account for marketing money as an investment? Is expenditure expected to generate a measurable return? If not, why not?

Review plans every time. It's just too easy to repeat last time's activity. Markets change, competition changes and you need to respond, or better still take the lead.

How can we improve accountability in our marketing and PR budgets? What could we put in place to increase our confidence levels?

12
We made the shortlist!

Improving the odds of winning a pitch

The shortlist is just the beginning – winning the business is the real prize. Put as much effort into closing the deal as you did to make the pitch list. Gather intelligence early: knowing what your competitors don't gives you a major edge.

Start building relationships long before the pitch and understand the client's decision-making process in advance. Choose your pitch team wisely, based on experience and proven success, and ensure everyone is rehearsed and prepared for any questions. Make sure nothing is overlooked.

The prize isn't making the shortlist, it's winning the business. Put at least as much effort into the second as the first.

Forward intelligence is critical in gaining advantage. If you know facts your competitors don't, that's a significant result. It's how battles and wars are won.

Build early relationships and always understand the client's decision-making process before the day of the pitch.

Improve the chances of a win by selecting a team based on their experience and track record. Don't forget to rehearse your roles and anticipate questions – it's obvious advice, but often overlooked.

13
Cross-selling

Theory to practice without losing your temper

Cross-selling can be a powerful strategy, but it starts with confirming there's real demand for the additional products or services you plan to offer. Assess your customer's buying behaviours to determine if they're the right fit for an expanded range.

Build a plan that takes your customer's needs into account and aligns with your internal processes and sales approach. Focus on accountability, incentivise your team, and be prepared for the shift in approach. It's certainly not easy, but with the right execution, cross-selling can lead to significant success.

OMG!! BUY- DON'T BUY! I AM SO OVER THIS!!!

He's an absolute master at cross selling...

Before you embark on any sort of cross-selling initiative, by bolting on extra products or services, establish evidence of demand.

Look at existing buying profiles. Would your current customer contact be the right buyer of an extended product range?

Construct a plan that recognises all the hurdles, from buyer demand (what problem are we solving for the customer?) to your own sales executives and internal management processes.

Target accountability and reward your executives. Cross-selling mostly fails because a complete restructure and new approach is required. However, when implemented, it mostly succeeds.

14
It's showtime!

High-impact seminars and events

Successful events begin with understanding what's current and what you want your brand to be known for. Plan your events at least a year ahead and build anticipation with timely invites and regular updates.

Hold speakers to high standards by managing their content, timing and Q&A to ensure a slick event. Provide valuable pre- and post-event networking opportunities. Follow up with every attendee and contact any no-shows. Neglecting this step is one of the main reasons event opportunities are missed.

What's coming up? What's topical?
What would you like to be known for?
Create a rolling document of ideas.
Plan a year of events and guarantee
all the associated marketing material
goes out on time.

Contact the invitees along the way with speaker updates. Build expectation.

Discipline your speakers on charts, messages, timing and Q&A. Under no circumstances give them an open brief and leave them to it. Create pre- and post-networking time.

Plan the follow-up as part of the event. Tell everyone there you're going to be in touch to discuss their own particular needs relating to the subject. Crucially, follow up with everyone: attendees, contacts and even those who didn't turn up. Without fail.

15
Getting to know you

How to look even more attractive

Building a network can be intimidating, with the fear of rejection holding many people back. But for those who know how, it creates golden opportunities. Preparation is key. Dedicate time to plan how to approach people, with a goal in mind.

Use the many tools available to build your database from current clients, contacts and LinkedIn. Offer them something relevant, well-researched and compelling, as this can make all the difference. It's all about them, not all about you.

Most people find network building very challenging. The fear of rejection looms large. This is an opportunity for those who know what to do.

Set quality time aside to plan the best way of getting in touch with people. There's a big prize at stake and you need to prepare.

There are plenty of tools available to build databases and client lists. It is relatively simple to create a network through current clients, contacts, LinkedIn and many other places.

*Generate curiosity and interest for
the person you want to meet. The
approach should be well researched,
relevant and compelling. Exclusive,
bespoke information or analysis
usually works and it doesn't have to
be lengthy or expensive.*

16
It could be love

Relationships that count for something

Building strong, genuine relationships is essential. Focus on deepening the connections you already have, while actively seeking out new opportunities to engage with others. Offer your help freely, without expecting anything in return – it's about creating goodwill.

When making introductions, be thoughtful. Connect people where there's real potential for mutual benefit, not just superficial compatibility. Over time, these efforts will build lasting value.

Relationships are the most important, precious thing you have in life. Look at what you have already and what you can do to strengthen and maintain your relationships.

New relationships occur for all sorts of reasons in all sorts of places. Improve your network by getting out more and being sincerely interested in and curious about other people.

Be generous in helping other people without always looking at it as a reciprocal arrangement. Good things will follow. You reap what you sow.

Make introductions by connecting people in your network. Be certain the reasons for doing this are real – not just because you think they'll get on. This is of great value and will be long remembered.

ORGANISATION

17
Sorry, I'm in a meeting

Spending time doing the right stuff

Before defaulting to fixing a meeting – internal or external – validate the purpose first. This will save both your time and everyone else's. Audit your company's meeting culture and challenge every meeting's purpose, decision-making process and expected outcomes.

Encourage a "Monday Revolution" mindset with fewer meetings, so those that happen are focused, decision-driven and efficient. The result? Meetings that are brief, purposeful and actually worth attending

⧗

Avoid arranging internal meetings as a default response. Don't agree to external meetings just because someone invites you to get together. Validate the purpose first. This will be good for both of you.

⏳

*Review your calendar and ask yourself
what the meeting is for and why you
need to be there. Do this as a quick-fire
exercise, withdraw from as many as
you can and limit your time at others.*

⏳

Audit company meetings. They'll thank you for it. Why are we meeting? What is the purpose? What will be decided? What will we do differently as a result of this meeting? Get useless meetings consigned to history.

⏳

Build a 'Monday Revolution' culture. "We don't have many internal meetings. We decided they're mostly a waste of time. The ones we do have are really focused on one or two key decisions and they never take too long. It's a real joy to attend."

18
I need help, with my help

Independent advice

When tackling persistent, long-standing issues, consider bringing in outside advice for a fresh perspective. However, this doesn't mean stepping back – it should be a collaborative effort, as implementation rests with you.

For independent advisors to be effective they must understand the unique culture and inner workings of your business. Provide access to the relevant people in your company, as a transparent, collaborative approach will lead to the best outcomes.

Consider using outside, independent advice, particularly for deep-seated problems that have remained unsolved for too long.

Outsourcing to help solve challenging problems should be collaborative. It's still your responsibility to get it fixed and you need to be fully engaged.

Independent advisors should provide advice within the context of your business. Therefore, they need access to a broad group of individuals to understand the culture and rules of your company.

Treat the engagement as a partnership
seeking a common goal. A healthy
relationship based on candour will
triumph, but recognise there will be
occasional healthy conflict between
you along the way.

19
Fast digital

Mandatory transformation. No exceptions

Digital transformation is no longer a luxury – it's essential for survival and growth. Maintaining and upgrading your technology and skill set is a must, not a luxury: it's a fundamental expectation from both customers and employees.

At the leadership level, digital knowledge is critical. Don't just keep up with digital advancements – be proactive and develop a clear investment plan. Embrace digital innovation as a key driver of business growth and a competitive advantage.

Being a digitally transformed company is now necessary for survival and growth. Upgrading tech is no longer a nice-to-have – users expect it.

Digital knowledge is mandatory at the top level. You're in charge. What do you know and what do you need to learn – quickly?

What digital data are you generating and how is it managed? Who is responsible for interpretation and making recommendations to identify commercial opportunities?

What's the digital investment plan? You need to do more than just keep up.

20
How did that happen?

Screw-ups and left-field moments

You can't afford to wait for a crisis to hit; be prepared before things go wrong. Keep a sharp eye on your key business lines and set up a system that flags risks early. Stay ahead of your suppliers by understanding their financial situation, not just your own.

You should always have a plan in place, even when the signs of trouble are not obvious. As necessary, make the tough changes and improvements to your company before external factors force you to respond. By then it will probably be too late.

seriously? A crash mat? That's it? That's your contingency plan?

Review and agree the critical business lines. Put a risk-monitoring system in place. Make sure the alarm is switched on.

Ensure essential suppliers can continue to supply. This means understanding their financial business model and accounts, not just your own.

Recognise there is no steady state.
You are expected to have a plan
even though the crisis may be
less than obvious.

Behave as a predator would and make
the changes and improvements to your
company before they do.

21
Deft decisions

Evidence–based. Always.

While intuition and experience are invaluable, they should always be backed by facts. Start by identifying areas where you already use evidence, then apply that approach to other aspects of your business.

Take a critical look at your decision-making processes – are they structured or ad hoc? Build a system that requires evidence at every step. Over time, this will shift your organisation towards a more data-driven culture, providing a powerful way of ensuring your decisions are rooted in solid facts.

I just feel like all this 'evidence' is getting in the way of you making the decision I want...

Try introducing a culture of evidence-based decision-making (assuming you don't have one). Support intuition and experience with facts.

Identify examples of where you currently use evidence and apply the principle to other areas. Review your formal decision-making processes – do you have any?

Build a requirement for evidence into the decision-making process. You will change to an evidence-based culture over time.

Mitigate decision bias before deciding.

Always ask: "How do we really know?"

GROWING

22
I want one of those!

Acquisitions

Acquisitions aren't always a quick fix for growth. Prior to closing a deal, review successful case studies and acquisition examples and apply those same principles to your business. Remember, most deals don't create value; they destroy it.

Don't underestimate the complexity of integrating new systems, cultures and synergies. Be cautious when dealing with advisors. Their focus is typically transaction-driven, and they don't carry long-term responsibility for the deal's success. Structure their fees to reflect the full value, not just the close.

Ok - so, it may or may not work out but the important thing is _we_ still get paid...

Growing your company should not rely on ad hoc acquisitions, however tempting. Obtain examples and case studies of where acquisitions in similar situations have worked well. Employ the same principles and metrics.

Advisors have a transaction-driven agenda. Mostly they do not have your best interests at heart. They carry little responsibility for the deal beyond the initial transaction.

Structure their fees to reflect the full benefits of the transaction – not just getting it done.

Unless your company is designed for acquisition – such as a private equity business, whose sole remit is deploying risk capital – recognise the risks involved in what can be unfamiliar territory. I'm not saying don't do deals. Just be careful.

Don't underestimate the challenge of integrating systems and cultures. Employ expertise to help before the deal is done.

23
Buried treasure

Discovering a new business in your business

Look within to uncover what makes your business truly unique. What are you doing already that could be developed and scaled to fuel future growth?

Continuously engage with your customers to identify opportunities for improvement or areas where you can offer something new. Technology is key to scaling your success and driving recurring revenue. Consider how you can adapt your current products and services.

*Start with what you're already
doing and identify the things in your
company you believe are unique to
you. This could be your buried treasure.*

Constantly ask groups of customers or clients what you could do better or supply what you currently don't. Invest in intelligent processes to identify insightful data you can action.

Tech is where you create scale. This is the holy grail. Repeat predictable revenues. What are you doing that could be adapted to fit this model?

Lead from the front. Personally sell the product yourself. First-hand experience enables better team reviews and much quicker improvements for the customer.

24
Who's your friend?

Partnerships and pitfalls

Partnerships can be a minefield. When tying your brand to another, ensure you have full control over the quality and service they provide. Don't risk your reputation for quick wins. When two companies collaborate, the weaker reputation always overshadows the stronger one and that will dominate both organisations.

Conduct thorough testing and make sure your contract includes a solid exit clause for underperformance. Make sure you protect your own interests.

Partnerships are tricky. When you lend your brand to someone else, be sure you can control the quality and service. Don't risk your reputation on their delivery.

Don't sacrifice reputation for the lure of short-term revenues and profits. "Don't take any wooden nickels when you sell your soul." When two companies come together, it is the reputation of the worst that prevails.

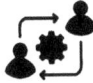

*Their reputation will stick to you
and yours to them. Make sure the
contract has an exit clause for
underperformance.*

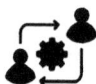

Carry out sufficient testing with due diligence and build in safeguards. Ensure the early days provide a low-profile escape route should it be required.

25
Three-year plans and other nonsense

The tyranny of prediction

Start with a brutally honest assessment of where your business stands today. Agree on clear baseline metrics. Workstreams are useful, but they aren't enough – identify the interdependencies and set priorities based on how everything connects.

Build a strategic plan with clear accountability: who's responsible for what, and by when? Regular reviews are key. It's easier to manage the plan's progress by keeping goals achievable with small, incremental steps.

In these unpredictable, volatile times we need a three-year plan...

Just a plan for tomorrow would be something...

Plans require a brutally honest appraisal of the business today. Agree the baseline metrics.

Separate workstreams are fine but they're not enough on their own. Work out interdependencies (what relies on what?) to set priorities. Join up thinking and action.

Build a plan which requires personal responsibility for what needs to happen by when and schedule frequent reviews. "What will you do by when? On a scale from one to ten how likely are you to succeed?" If the answer is less than 9, work together to improve the odds.

Keep tasks within reach. Small steps
are far more effective than big leaps.
No time like the present.

LISTENING
AND
LEARNING

26
Listening

You can choose – fast or slow

Poor listening is all too common and often goes unnoticed.
Whether it's forgetting names, interrupting others or
failing to fully engage in conversations, these habits can
hinder effective communication.

Fast-paced environments may encourage us to rush
through interactions, but active listening is key to building
trust, understanding perspectives and making better
decisions. The best listeners aren't just hearing – they're
engaged, curious and willing to be present in the moment.

There are many reasons we don't listen. All of them understandable if not excusable. Developing great listening skills takes practice, patience and time. It is one of the most rewarding and influential things you can ever do. It should be taught in schools. Read Nancy Kline, who will tell you what to do to improve.

*Always listen to the reply to your
question. Then ask another.*

*People reveal astonishingly interesting
information unexpectedly. After asking
how they are, ask why that is!*

While listening to someone speak, never look away. Particularly at social events when you've concluded you're wasting your time. Commit to being present.

If you realise the person you're talking to has stopped listening to what you're saying, pause and the silence will bring them back. It works.

27
Great communication

Say nothing

Good communicators listen first. They remain silent. They don't interrupt. They speak to confirm or clarify what has been said. They only respond when others have finished. This is leadership at its most powerful.

Try to go last, not first in your meetings. Practise being present, especially in moments when it's tempting to tune out. Ask follow-up questions, dig deeper and embrace the silence when needed. Give your full attention and it can pay off in every conversation.

OK, we're both obviously great at the silence/listening thing... but at some point one of us should actually speak...

The most successful leaders and executives often say the least. They listen and respond. They do not dive in.

🔇✕

Leaders often feel there is an expectation they should always go first. Open the meeting, set the tone or challenge the room. Sometimes that's right, but not every time. Instead ask for views without expressing your own, and stay silent.

Great negotiators know that when they remain silent, the other person eventually feels the need fill the silence, often conceding an important point. Stay quiet and hold your nerve.

🔇✕

Remaining silent can be interpreted as displeasure or disagreement. If this isn't your intent, pre-empt your silence by saying it is an important point which you want a few moments to consider.

28
Everyday practice

Listening skills

Focus on understanding, not self-comparing. Avoid turning every conversation into a chance to share your own experiences or perspectives. Try a day without offering an opinion, advice, anecdote or story. Ask a question and just listen. Struggling with names or claiming a low attention span signals poor listening skills – don't make excuses!

Use everyday interactions to practise active listening. Ask more thoughtful questions and engage meaningfully, even in brief encounters. It's a simple way to improve your listening in real-world situations.

Practise not responding with a similar story or anecdote to the one you're listening to. Instead ask a question to find out more.

*Saying you're no good at remembering
names is a weakness best not shared.
It's a sign of poor listening.*

Saying you have a low boredom threshold isn't a sign of intelligence. It's symptomatic of a poor listener.

Select a person in your everyday life with whom you can practise listening by asking questions. Not in a meeting, but in a shop, coffee place or on a train, for example. Choose anyone you could naturally interact with but would not usually get further than asking "How are you?"

29
Hanging out in the zone of comfort

Your choice

We spend most of our time avoiding learning. The comfort zone is, well, more comfortable. Real learning happens when deliberate or accidental challenge arrives. Next time something you find too hard shows up, take it on.

Embrace a mindset of daily learning. It can transform even the most mundane tasks into opportunities for growth. Look at events you dread and find ways to learn from them. Challenge your team to share what they've learnt each day – it'll soon become second nature.

OK! LET'S GET STARTED... AND I'VE PROMISED MYSELF I'LL **LEARN** SOMETHING AND **NOT** FIND YOU ALL TERMINALLY BORING...

Daily learning can be a mindset that is rewarding and fun. It can turn tedious events into something worthwhile.

Take a regular event you're least looking forward to and think what you could learn from attending. My personal favourite was asking a question every ten minutes at an audit meeting. I learnt a lot.

Challenge your team by asking what they learnt today. They will soon get into the habit, knowing that the question is coming.

Consider what you could learn that you currently depend on others to do for you. This will be a long list…

30
Finding out more

Is it really that hard?

Face value? Try asking a second or third question. Curiosity and interest are skills to develop at any age. Asking simple questions can open doors to knowledge you've never considered.

And don't forget the value of teaching others – sharing your knowledge is not only rewarding, but it also reinforces your own learning. And when you are genuinely interested people respond in all sorts of unpredictable ways. Because others rarely ask....

?

"How does that work?" is a great question to ask and can spark deeper conversations. Never underestimate the power of curiosity.

When you show interest in other people's skills, they often offer to teach you. And sometimes a whole new world opens up…

All knowledge is available to learn from your digital devices. Everything is just a click away, from tutorials to online courses. No excuses now.

Share what you know to help others learn. It's rewarding.

Teaching is one of the best ways to solidify your own knowledge.

THE LAST
WORD

Throughout this book, I've shared my belief in what works to try and help others avoid mistakes I've made. The actions weren't part of a linear process, but more often a case of trial and error. I could have written a larger, equivalent volume on all I've done that didn't work out. Maybe that will be my third attempt at publishing!

Much of our lives are dictated by events and circumstances that were impossible to predict, leaving us to reflect on how we coped and perhaps what we might have done better or differently.

Knowledge sharing is a nascent activity. Too often, if we'd only had an experienced guide, mentor or coach, we might have made a better, more informed decision. Or have been better able to cope with those unexpected moments.

My last word is to encourage you to share what you've learnt. In your friendship circle, there will be those who'd welcome your experience. Young people, particularly, need support and often are at a loss to know where to find it. Older people, too, as they progress through the years, will be confronting new challenges without knowing the answers.

Look around. You already know these people. Use your mistakes and successes to help. This is your final action point. And you can start the Revolution on Monday!

Good luck!
David

DAVID MANSFIELD, founder of *The Monday Revolution*, advises organisations on decision-making, business simplification and rapid-growth strategies. His leadership experience includes roles at Capital Radio, Carphone Warehouse and RAJAR. He offers practical expertise and is dedicated to helping leaders navigate complex business environments.

David holds a master's in Strategic Decision-Making and is pursuing a doctorate in Business Administration at Cranfield University, furthering his insights into organisational success. As a respected business leader, speaker and coach, he has guided many leaders and teams to rethink their work approaches, focusing on what truly matters to achieve transformational results.

Enjoyed this book?
Discover the first in the series!

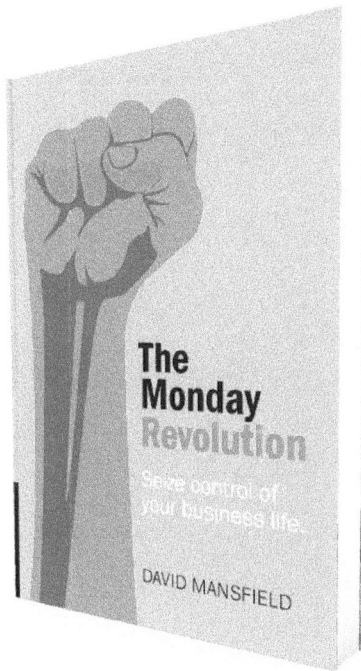

"Less a business book and more a series of captivating stories that give brilliant lessons for being more effective and successful at work. A fantastic page turning read!"

BRUCE DAISLEY – VICE PRESIDENT, EMEA, TWITTER

"Packed with stories, case studies and immediate actions you can take NOW, this book is a must read, whether you're running an established company or building a new enterprise."

PAUL LINDLEY – FOUNDER, ELLA'S KITCHEN

Find out more and get your copy here: